Twenty

Stitched Fabric
Brooches

Alex McQuade

Search Press

First published in 2014

Search Press Limited
Wellwood, North Farm Road,
Tunbridge Wells, Kent TN2 3DR

Text copyright © Alex McQuade 2014

Photographs by Paul Bricknell
at Search Press Studios

Photographs and design copyright
© Search Press Ltd 2014

ISBN: 978-1-78221-040-5

Suppliers
If you have difficulty in obtaining any of the
materials and equipment mentioned in this
book, then please visit the Search Press website
for details of suppliers: www.searchpress.com

Printed in China

Dedication
In memory of my Mum, who first
introduced me to the creative
world of art and textiles.

Acknowledgements
A huge thank you to my husband
Chris for all his help in making my
dreams a reality, and thank you to
the fantastic team at Search Press
for making this book possible.

Publisher's Note
For further information you are
invited to visit the author's website:
www.alexmcquade.co.uk

Contents

Introduction

I was introduced to a wide variety of textile techniques at an early age, but it wasn't until my final year of studying textile design at university that I created my first brooch. Bizarrely, the inspiration came from some vintage tractors! Although it may seem a strange source of inspiration, it was the patterns and textures that caught my attention, especially those found on the wheels. You can find design ideas almost anywhere, you just need to keep your eyes and mind open, and this is what I love most about creating fabric brooches, badges and corsages.

Something that's really important to me and helps me achieve a wide range of results is to keep hold of old textile items or clothing. Not only is this great because recycling is good and up-cycling is a bit trendy, but it also helps to save money! In no time at all you can build up a collection of fabrics, buttons and ribbons, and because of the size of the projects in this book, you often only need small pieces of fabric to create the most fabulous outcomes. I also love vintage style, so anything passed down from relatives is always greatly appreciated and adds an extra-special feel to the items created.

This book includes a wide range of projects, which are diverse in style, materials and techniques. It includes quirky brooches you can wear every day, beautiful bridal corsages and lots of simple-to-make but elaborate-looking projects designed to be a statement piece on any jacket! I hope you find them inspiring, fun to create and a pleasure to wear. Enjoy!

Techniques

The projects in this book use a number of simple hand stitches, which are shown below. As well as these there is a number of useful techniques to know: free machine embroidery is used throughout as it gives a wonderful quirkiness to your brooches; an embroidery hoop will keep your fabric taut as you stitch; and once you've made up your brooches you will need to attach a brooch finding so that they can be worn.

Back stitch

Running stitch

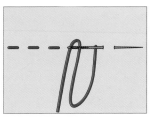

Seed stitch

Stab stitch

French knots

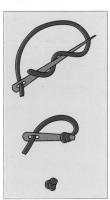

Oversewing

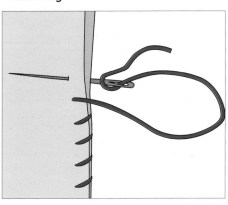

Blanket stitch

Couching stitch

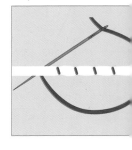

Using an embroidery hoop

Whenever possible, it is best to secure your fabric in an embroidery hoop – this keeps the fabric taut, while the edges of the hoop allow you to easily hold and keep control of your work. When using your embroidery hoop for machine stitching you will need to use it 'upside down'. Lay the fabric over the outer hoop with the right side facing up, then push the inner hoop on top. When you come to sew, your fabric will sit flat on the needle plate.

Free machine embroidery

This technique allows you to use the sewing machine like a drawing tool as you can move the fabric under the needle in any direction. In most cases, all you have to do is set the machine to a straight stitch, attach a darning foot and drop the feed dog (but do check your machine's instructions). Practice makes perfect with this technique: working through basic shapes such as circles, squares and triangles is a great way to start and will soon build up your confidence. The charm of this style is that you'll never create two identical pieces and they're unlikely to look exactly like mine – each design will have its own quirky character.

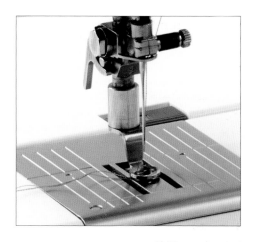

Attaching a brooch finding

Cut a circle of fabric – appropriate to the size of the project – and stitch a brooch finding just above the centre point. Use strong thread that tones with the colour of your fabric, and hand sew through the finding's holes until it is secure. Then, either stitch the circular fabric to the rear of the project using blanket stitch – making sure that your stitching only catches the rear layer or layers of fabric and is not visible from the front of the brooch – or attach it using a glue gun.

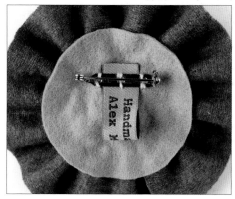

Using cover buttons to create a badge

You don't need a badge machine to make a badge – you can easily create one using a metal cover button. Simply remove the button shank from the cover button with a pair of pliers and then cover the button with fabric as per the instructions. Attach the cover button back and then simply secure an appropriate brooch finding to the back using a craft glue gun. Cover buttons come in a range of sizes, so choose one appropriate to your project.

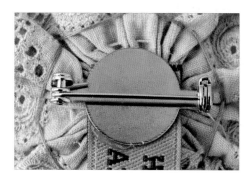

Ribbon Badge

Materials:

Neutral-coloured lightweight fabric, cotton or calico, 14 x 14cm (5½ x 5½in)

Lace

Machine thread

Badge blank (if using a badge machine) or a 30mm (1¼in) metal cover button

Ribbon, two colours

Brooch finding

Tools:

Embroidery hoop, 10cm (4in)

Fabric scissors

Sewing machine

Badge machine (optional)

Pliers (if using a metal cover button)

Hand sewing needle

Craft glue gun

Instructions:

1 Secure the neutral-coloured fabric in the embroidery hoop – use the hoop 'upside down' (see page 7), so that the fabric can sit directly on the needle plate of your machine.

2 Cut a circular piece of lace: use either the manufacturer's guide for size if using a badge machine, or the instructions provided if using a metal cover button. Place the circle of fabric in the centre of the embroidery hoop.

3 Prepare your machine for the free machine embroidery technique described on page 7, and position the hoop under your darning foot. In a complementary thread colour, sew a decorative spiral pattern starting at the centre and working out to the edge of the lace circle.

4 Take the fabric out of the hoop and cut around the lace circle.

5 If you are using a badge machine, follow the manufacturer's instructions using the embroidered lace circle. If you are using a metal cover button, remove the button shank with a pair of pliers and discard. Carefully fold the fabric around the button, following the instructions. Once in place, secure the cover button back but don't attach the brooch finding.

6 Cut a length of lace 25cm (10in) long and about 2.5cm (1in) wide. Take a piece of thread, double it over and tie a double knot in the end. Hand sew a small running stitch along the entire length of lace, approximately 0.5cm (¼in) from the edge; stitch along the less decorative edge if the piece of lace has one.

7 Once you have stitched to the end, gather the lace by pulling the two ends of the thread together; manipulate the lace to create a tightly gathered circle. Tie the two thread ends together with a double knot to secure. Attach this to the rear of the badge using either tiny stab stitches through the lace and edge of the badge or by using a little glue from a craft glue gun.

8 Cut two lengths of ribbon, one 12cm (5in) long and one 10cm (4in) long. Fold each ribbon at the centre point to create an upside down 'V' shape. Attach them to the rear of the badge using a little glue; secure the shorter ribbon first, then glue the longer ribbon. Trim the ends at an angle to prevent fraying.

9 Secure a brooch finding to the rear with glue.

Grandma's lace

Experiment with different ribbons and types of lace. Ask your relatives if they have anything hidden away in boxes. I was lucky enough to be given lots of beautiful lace that originally belonged to my husband's great grandma Lillian. It gives extra meaning to the brooch and I treasure it dearly.

9

Bird Badge

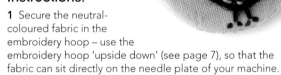

Materials:

Neutral-coloured lightweight fabric, cotton or calico, 14 x 14cm (5½ x 5½in)

Coloured lightweight fabric, cotton or calico

Coloured felt

Embroidery threads

Machine thread

Badge blank (if using a badge machine) or a 30mm (1¼in) metal cover button

Brooch finding

Metallic acrylic paint

Tools:

Embroidery hoop, 10cm (4in)

Fabric scissors

Embroidery needle

Sewing machine

Badge machine (optional)

Pliers (if using a metal cover button)

Craft glue gun

Cocktail stick

Instructions:

1 Secure the neutral-coloured fabric in the embroidery hoop – use the embroidery hoop 'upside down' (see page 7), so that the fabric can sit directly on the needle plate of your machine.

2 Cut a circle of coloured lightweight fabric: use either the manufacturer's guide for size if using a badge machine, or the instructions provided if using a metal cover button. Place the circle of fabric onto the centre of the embroidery hoop.

3 Using the template on page 48, cut out a felt bird and place in the centre of the circle of fabric.

4 Using back stitch, hand sew around the inside edge of the bird shape.

5 Using a brown embroidery thread, hand sew a few simple seed stitches to create the bird's legs and feet.

6 Prepare your sewing machine for free machine embroidery (see page 7) and position the embroidery hoop under the darning foot. Sew a circle of stitches around the entire bird design – the circle should have a diameter of about 3cm (1¼in), as it will sit close to the edge of the badge.

7 Take the fabric out of the embroidery hoop and cut around the circle of fabric created in step two.

8 If you are using a badge machine, follow the manufacturer's instructions for constructing the badge. If you are using a metal cover button, remove the button shank with a pair of pliers and discard. Then carefully fold the fabric around the button, following the instructions. Once in place, secure the cover button back and glue a brooch back to the rear using a glue gun.

9 Add the bird's little eye by applying a dot of metallic acrylic paint in place with the end of a cocktail stick.

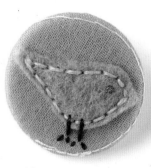

Cute and quirky

Be playful with your colours – experiment with lots of different fabrics and threads. Think about the accessories you own, too, as these little badges look great pinned to bags and purses as well as jackets and hats.

Heart Badge

Materials:

Neutral-coloured lightweight fabric, cotton or calico, 14 x 14cm (5½ x 5½in)

Coloured lightweight fabric, cotton or calico

Pink felt

Embroidery threads

Badge blank (if using a badge machine) or a 30mm (1¼in) metal cover button

Brooch finding

Tools:

Embroidery hoop, 10cm (4in)

Fabric scissors

Embroidery needle

Badge machine (optional)

Pliers (if using a metal cover button)

Craft glue gun

Instructions:

1 Secure the neutral-coloured lightweight fabric in the embroidery hoop.

2 Cut a circle of coloured lightweight fabric: use either the manufacturer's guide for size if using a badge machine, or the instructions provided if using a metal cover button. Place the circle of fabric onto the centre of the embroidery hoop.

3 Using the template on page 48, cut out a heart shape from a piece of felt and place in the centre of the circle of fabric.

4 Using a contrasting thread colour, hand sew back stitch around the inside edge of the heart, pushing the needle through all three layers of fabric.

5 Using running stitch, carefully sew a dashed circle around the heart shape – the circle should have a diameter of about 3cm (1¼in), as it will sit right on the edge of the badge.

6 With your stitching complete, take the fabric out of the embroidery hoop and cut around the coloured circle of fabric.

7 If you are using a badge machine, follow the manufacturer's instructions to construct the badge. If you are using a metal cover button, remove the button shank with a pair of pliers and discard. Carefully fold the fabric around the button, following the instructions. Once in place, secure the cover button back and glue a brooch back to the rear using a glue gun.

Vintage feel

Create a vintage look using a piece of old lace, soft colours and lovely French knots as the decorative outer stitch. These pretty little badges also make wonderful wedding favours at a vintage-themed wedding celebration.

Snail Badge

Materials:

Neutral-coloured lightweight fabric, cotton or calico, 14 x 14cm (5½ x 5½in)

Coloured lightweight fabric, cotton or calico

Embroidery threads

Badge blank (if using a badge machine) or a 30mm (1¼in) metal cover button

Boiled wool

Thin cord

Brooch finding

Tools:

Embroidery hoop, 10cm (4in)

Fabric scissors

Embroidery needle

Badge machine (optional)

Pliers (if using a metal cover button)

Craft glue gun

Instructions:

1 Secure the neutral-coloured fabric in the embroidery hoop.

2 Cut a circle of coloured lightweight fabric: use either the manufacturer's guide for size if using a badge machine, or the instructions provided if using a metal cover button. Place the circle of fabric onto the centre of the embroidery hoop.

3 Using the embroidery thread and starting at the centre point of the circle, hand sew a spiral design using a back stitch; start at the centre and stop when you reach the outer edge of the circle.

4 Using a different thread colour, add a few simple seed stitches along the spiral for extra decoration.

5 Take the fabric out of the hoop and cut out the circle of fabric.

6 If you are using a badge machine, follow the manufacturer's instructions to construct the badge. If you are using a metal cover button, remove the button shank with a pair of pliers and discard. Carefully fold the fabric around the button, following the instructions. Once in place, secure the cover button back but do not yet attach the badge or brooch finding.

7 Using a double layer of boiled wool, cut out a body shape for the snail – on the piece that will form the top layer, include a circular area on top for the shell badge to sit on.

8 Cut a length of cord 4cm (1½in) long for the antennae.

9 Stitch around the edge of the body by oversewing the two layers together; at the top of the head, trap the centre point of the cord in an overstitch to secure the antennae in place.

10 Use brown embroidery thread to create a French knot eye.

11 Attach the shell badge to the body using a craft glue gun. Glue the brooch finding to the back of the shell.

Free machine fun

If your preference is machine embroidery rather than hand, try speeding things up with a free machine embroidered shell design. You could even go a little crazy with the pattern you make or colours you use. This will reduce the making time and looks just as good!

15

Recycled Fabric Brooch

Materials:

Decorative or recycled fabrics, five different types

Metal washer

Embroidery threads

Button

Brooch finding

Tools:

Pencil

Pair of compasses

Card

Paper scissors

Air-erasable pen

Fabric scissors

Ruler

Embroidery needle

> ### Tip: preserving your frayed edges
> You can buy products that will stop your edges from fraying too far. They come in liquid form and should be applied once you reach the frayed effect you want. However, always complete a fabric test first to make sure the product dries clear!

Instructions:

1 Using the pencil and pair of compasses, draw five circles on a piece of card: the diameters should measure about 5cm (2in), 5.5cm (2¹⁄₈in), 6cm (2¼in), 6.5cm (2½in) and 7cm (2¾in). Cut out the card circles to create your five templates.

2 Decide in which order you want your fabrics to appear, then place a template on each. Draw around each template using the air-erasable pen and then cut out five fabric circles.

3 Layer the circles on top of each other in order – largest at the bottom, smallest at the top.

4 Using the ruler, find the central point of the design and mark with the air-erasable pen. Place the metal washer in the middle of the design using the pen mark as a guide.

5 Using the embroidery thread, stitch the washer into place using a simple couching stitch around the metal ring.

6 Using the same thread, stitch an appropriately sized button over the centre of the washer.

7 Encourage the edges to fray a little by gently pulling at them.

8 Attach the brooch finding (see page 7).

Alternative edging

If you prefer a neater finish, try using a pair of pinking shears to cut out the fabric circles. You'll achieve an interesting look and prolong the life of the brooch.

Butterfly Brooch

Materials:

Felt fabric, two colours

Decorative fabric, two colours

Machine threads

Cord

Embroidery thread

Brooch finding

Tools:

Embroidery hoop,
  10cm (4in)

Paper scissors

Fabric scissors

Sewing machine

Dress pin

Embroidery needle

Tip: pattern perfection
Try to keep the patterns on each side of the butterfly symmetrical, as this will give a better overall finish – practise on scraps of fabric until you are confident.

Instructions:

1 Secure a piece of felt fabric in the embroidery hoop – this will form the upper felt layer – here, grey was used.

2 Using the templates on page 48 cut out the top and bottom wings of the butterfly using a different decorative fabric for each.

3 Using the embroidery hoop upside down (see page 7), position the butterfly's bottom wings in the hoop.

4 Using the free machine embroidery technique described on page 7 stitch a pretty pattern onto the wings to secure them in place: sew a tear-drop shaped loop across the centre of each wing and then sew a looping, scalloped line around each.

5 Place the top wings into the hoop so that they slightly overlap the bottom wings. Stitch around the inside edge of the top wings to secure them, then sew tear-drop shaped loops part way across the centre of each wing. Change the thread colour and stitch a circle at the tip of each top wing.

6 Take the design out of the hoop and cut around the butterfly leaving a 0.5cm (¼in) felt border.

7 Lay the design on another piece of felt that is larger than the butterfly – here, yellow was used. Secure the layers with a pin at the edge of the bottom right wing.

8 Cut a length of thin cord about 10cm (4in) long, which when folded in half will run up the length of the body and create two antennae at the top. Using a contrasting thread colour, hand sew the cord in place using about five evenly spaced couching stitches – make sure you push the needle through all the layers of fabric.

9 Being careful of the antennae, cut around the bottom layer of felt leaving a 0.5cm (¼in) felt border. Remove the pin.

10 Attach the brooch finding (see page 7).

18

Lacy layer

For something a little prettier, create a delicate effect by adding a lacy layer to the top wings. You could take this idea even further and use lighter weight fabrics instead of felts as your backing. Try to have fun and experiment – you may be surprised by the results!

Wire Heart Brooch

Materials:

Craft wire
Decorative fabric or felt
Embroidery threads
Base felt
Polyester filling
Brooch finding

Tools:

Long-nosed craft pliers
Fabric scissors
Air-erasable fabric pen
Dress pin
Embroidery needle

Instructions:

1 Cut a piece of craft wire approximately 15cm (6in) long, using the cutting tool on the craft pliers. Use the pliers to create an ornate, coiled heart shape – try to keep the ends of the wire folded in tightly to prevent them from catching on anything.

2 Place the wire heart onto the decorative fabric and using an air-erasable pen draw a heart shape around the wire that is 1cm (½in) larger all round. Cut out the fabric heart with scissors, following the pen line.

3 Place the fabric heart onto a piece of felt, inserting a pin through the centre to hold the two layers together. Position the wire back on top. Secure the wire in place using the embroidery thread and a couching stitch. Stitch the entire length of the wire going through both the fabric and felt layers. Remove the pin.

4 Cut around the decorative fabric heart, leaving a 1cm (½in) felt border.

5 Place the heart design on to another piece of felt, which will form the back of your brooch. Pin all the layers together, then cut around the heart shape again – this time leaving no border.

6 Starting at the top middle, use embroidery thread to hand sew a blanket stitch around the outside edge of the design, pausing when you are 3cm (1¼in) from your starting point. Remove the pin.

7 Fill the heart shape with a little polyester wadding then continue the blanket stich until the heart is stitched closed.

8 Attach the brooch finding (see page 7).

> **Tip: filling your heart**
> Less is more when it comes to adding the polyester filling. Insert it bit by bit, and use enough to make the heart three-dimensional, but not so much that it distorts the shape and becomes awkward to wear.

Stand-out style

Create something really unique with an adventurous wire design – use a longer piece of wire to make this double-layered heart. Choose bold and bright fabrics and threads and it's sure to stand out.

Cottage Brooch

Materials:

Lightweight fabric, cotton or calico, 14 x 14cm (5½ x 5½in)

Felt, two colours

Machine threads

Brooch finding

Tools:

Embroidery hoop, 10cm (4in)

Fabric scissors

Sewing machine

Instructions:

1 Secure a piece of lightweight fabric in the embroidery hoop.

2 Using the templates on page 48 cut out the rectangle and roof shapes using a different felt colour for each.

3 Place the rectangular shape into the upside down embroidery hoop (see page 7).

4 Using free machine embroidery and starting at the top left of the rectangle, sew around the inside edge of the rectangle twice, adding a door detail on your second circuit.

5 Once complete, lift the machine foot and cut the thread. Using the same technique, stitch the four windows, remembering to lift the foot at the end of each and snip the thread.

6 Take the fabric roof shape and place it in position just overlapping the main part of the cottage. Stitch around the inside edge of the roof shape twice to secure it in place.

7 Take the design out of the embroidery hoop and cut around the design leaving a 1cm (½in) lightweight fabric border.

8 Place the design onto a larger piece of coloured felt – here grey was used to match the roof – and set the sewing machine to do a standard zigzag stitch. Starting at the bottom, stitch around the entire edge of the design, ensuring that the stitch sits half on the lightweight fabric and half on the felt.

9 Cut around the bottom layer of felt leaving about a 3mm (⅛in) border, making sure you keep the overall cottage shape.

10 Attach the brooch finding (see page 7).

> ### Tip: choosing threads
> Make sure you use a thread colour that is much darker than the fabrics when you come to embroider the cottage. You want to make sure the outline, door and windows stand out.

Stylish stitching

If you are confident with free machine embroidery, add your own style to the piece with a fancy edging stitch. This sample shows a straight stitch around the edge, staying very close to the cottage design, and then an additional wave-like stitch around the edge of the cotton.

Folded Fabric Brooch

Materials:

Decorative fabrics, four types
Cotton thread
Small button
Extra small button
Embroidery thread
Brooch finding

Tools:

Card
Pencil
Pair of compasses
Paper scissors
Air-erasable pen
Fabric scissors
Embroidery needle

Instructions:

1 Using the pencil and pair of compasses, draw a circle on the card with a 7cm (2¾in) diameter. Cut out to create your template.

2 Create eight fabric circles, two from each fabric – draw around the template with the air-erasable pen and then cut out.

3 Lay the circles out in front of you so that you have two columns of four – make sure you have one of each fabric type in each column and make sure the two closest to you are the most decorative as these will create the top of the brooch.

4 Starting at the top of the left-hand column, pick up the fabric and fold it in half. Using the sewing needle and a double length of cotton, knotted at the end, begin to oversew along the fold – space the stitches out and create about six in total. Stay very close to the fold (the effect is a little like book binding).

5 Working your way down and then back up the columns, pick up the next piece of fabric, fold it in half and place directly on top of the last. This time oversew the first piece of fabric and second piece together, as close to the folded edge as possible.

6 Fold the third piece of fabric and place it directly on top of the last one. This time when you oversew along the folded edges, only go through this new piece of fabric and the previous one.

7 Continue with this technique for all of the circular pieces until you reach the last piece: the top right of the second column.

8 Find the central two fabrics and open the brooch out like a book so that they each form half of the brooch top.

9 Using the embroidery needle and thread sew a decorative button at the central point and then stitch a cute little button on the top right hand side.

10 Attach the brooch finding (see page 7).

Bright and bold

This is a quirky little design that looks great in both soft, subtle colours and brighter, bolder shades. With a slight change to the size – try making a template with a 4cm (1½in) diameter – this design makes a cute addition to a hair band or hair clips.

Shimmer and Shine Brooch

Materials:

Felt

Sequins, two colours

Small beads

Beading thread

Embroidery thread

Small button,
   diameter about 1.5cm (½in)

Brooch finding

Tools:

Pencil

Card

Craft scissors

Fabric scissors

Beading needle

Ruler

Embroidery needle

Instructions:

1 Using a pencil on card, draw out a heart shape that is approximately 7cm (2¾in) tall and 5cm (2in) wide. Cut this out to create your template. Using this template, cut out two identical heart shapes from coloured felt.

2 Lay one piece on top of the other, aligning them exactly, and pin them together – use one pin in the centre of the shape.

3 Using the beading needle and thread, stitch a row of sequins and beads around the outer edge of the heart. To do this, bring the needle up through both layers of fabric, thread a sequin through the needle and position the sequin in place. Then thread a bead through the needle and insert the needle back through the sequin hole and fabric layers. This will secure the sequin and bead. Continue this all the way around the edge, slightly overlapping each sequin to create a neat finish.

4 Use the ruler to find the centre point of the heart and stitch a small decorative button in place using bright embroidery thread.

5 Using the technique described in step three, add another line of darker, slightly smaller sequins between the outer sequins and the central button.

6 Add a few beads to the space left between the central button and the inner sequins.

7 Attach the brooch finding (see page 7).

Shape up!
You could adapt this design to any basic shape – why not try a circle? The sparkle and flair of the sequins works well with the simplicity of the shape.

Dog Brooch

Materials:

Dog-coloured felt
Embroidery thread
Polyester filling
Ribbon
Button
Brooch finding

Tools:

Fabric scissors
Embroidery needle

Instructions:

1 Using the template on page 48, cut out two dog body shapes from the coloured felt.

2 Lay one piece on top of the other, aligning them perfectly, and secure them in the centre with a pin.

3 Starting at the top of the tail and moving anti-clockwise, hand sew a blanket stitch around the outer edge. Pause when you reach the bottom of the dog's back leg. Remove the pin.

4 Stuff the shape with a little polyester filling and continue the blanket stitch until the dog is stitched closed.

5 Cut a length of ribbon 12.5cm (5in) long and cut one end at a sharp diagonal angle. Thread the button onto the ribbon.

6 Place the ribbon around the dog's neck and secure it at the back with a double knot. Cut off any excess ribbon, snipping the ends at an angle to prevent them from fraying.

7 Attach the brooch finding (see page 7).

> **Tip: filling your dog**
> Use a knitting needle or pencil to insert the polyester wadding; use only very small amounts at a time and you will fill the shape more evenly.

Personalised pooch
Try using different colours and button shapes to change the look and personalise the brooch. Or try adding a bell to create a lovely festive brooch for Christmas time!

Holly Brooch

Materials:

Lightweight fabric, cotton or calico, 20 x 20cm (8 x 8in)

Decorative green and brown fabrics

Red felt

Machine threads

Double-sided tape

Hessian fabric

Neutral-coloured felt

Embroidery thread

Red buttons

Brooch finding

Tools:

Medium embroidery hoop, 15cm (6in)

Fabric scissors

Sewing machine

Embroidery needle

Instructions:

1 Secure a piece of lightweight fabric in the embroidery hoop.

2 Using the templates on page 48, cut out two outer leaf shapes from brown fabric, two inner leaf shapes from green fabric, and the berries from red felt.

3 With the hoop upside down (see page 7), place the leaf shapes on the lightweight fabric, outer shapes first and the inner shapes on top. Make sure the leaves have plenty of space around them – they shouldn't be overlapping at this stage.

4 Using green thread, free machine embroider a leaf pattern onto both leaves: stitch around the inner leaf edge twice and up the centre to the tip and back down.

5 Take the designs out of the embroidery hoop and cut out each of the leaf shapes, leaving a border of lightweight fabric just under 1cm (½in) wide.

6 Apply a little double-sided tape to the back of each leaf and place them onto a piece of hessian. Cut around each shape leaving a border of hessian just under 1cm (½in) wide.

7 Place each leaf onto a piece of neutral-coloured felt. Using the sewing machine, free machine embroider the outline of the leaf shape on the lightweight fabric. Make sure the needle passes through the lightweight fabric, the hessian and the felt layer. Repeat for the other leaf. Cut the leaves out but do not leave a felt border.

8 Position the two leaves so that one slightly overlaps the other. Using about four stitches, sew them together at the back – be careful not to stitch through all of the layers as you don't want to see the stitches from the front. Position the felt berries shape created at step two and add about four more stitches at the back to secure it in place.

9 Using red embroidery thread, sew three little red buttons to the berries shape – they do not need to match.

10 Attach the brooch finding (see page 7).

Faster foliage

For a quicker result, at step three, place all the pieces in their overlapped position in the embroidery hoop. Free machine embroider in place so that you have only one shape to cut out. These versatile designs look great with a little jute string added and hung on the Christmas tree. Using the same method you could also make a mistletoe design to hang over a door!

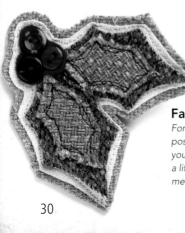

Bird Brooch

Materials:

Coloured felt,
    14 x 14cm (5½ x 5½in)

Decorative fabrics, two types

Embroidery threads

Polyester filling

Two beads

Thin cord

Brooch finding

Tools:

Embroidery hoop,
    10cm (4in)

Fabric scissors

Embroidery needle

Dress pin

Instructions:

1 Secure the piece of felt in the embroidery hoop.

2 Using the template on page 48 cut a bird shape from one of the decorative fabrics.

3 Place the bird shape onto the embroidery hoop and using the embroidery thread, hand sew a running stitch around the inner edge of the entire body – here, blue thread was used.

4 Using the wing template on page 48 cut a wing out of the second decorative fabric, carefully position it as shown, then hand sew it onto your bird body using a back stitch.

5 Take the fabric out of the hoop and cut around the bird design leaving a 1cm (½in) border of the base felt.

6 Place the design onto another piece of felt, insert a pin through the centre of all the layers to secure them in place and cut around the bird shape again, this time leaving no border.

7 Starting at the beak and working clockwise, hand sew a blanket stitch around the edge of the bird, pausing just after you have reached the lowest point – this should leave an opening about 3cm (1¼in) long. Remove the pin.

8 Carefully stuff the bird with a little polyester filling then continue the blanket stitch until the bird has been stitched closed. Secure the thread neatly.

9 Add a French knot for an eye. Push the needle through all the layers – don't pull too tight or the fabric will pucker.

10 To create the legs, cut a piece of cord 10cm (4in) long and tie a knot at one end. Thread two beads onto the cord then tie a knot at the other end. Trim the ends so that the knots are the same distance from each end.

11 Fold the cord in half, with one bead at each end, and tuck the fold under the bird's body. Secure the legs by sewing a couple of couching stitches over the fold.

12 Attach the brooch finding (see page 7).

Soft touch

Play around with different colour combinations until you get the look you want. You may like to try more subtle, soft colours – just make sure you pick a colour for the wing that stands out from the body.

Tractor Wheel Brooch

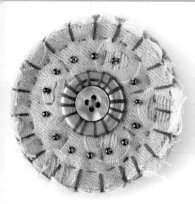

Materials:

Decorative fabric

Wadding

Felt

Scrim

Metal washer

Embroidery threads

Beads

Beading thread

Small button

Brooch finding

Tools:

Pair of compasses

Pencil

Card

Paper scissors

Air-erasable pen

Fabric scissors

Ruler

Embroidery needle

Beading needle

Instructions:

1 Using the pencil and pair of compasses, draw a circle on the card that has a 7cm (2¾in) diameter. Cut out to create your template.

2 Place the template on your decorative fabric, draw around it using the air-erasable pen, then cut out a fabric circle. Repeat for the wadding and felt. Place the template on a piece of scrim and cut roughly around it, making it 1cm (½in) larger all round.

3 Stack the circles: felt at the bottom, then wadding, then scrim and finally the decorative fabric on top.

4 Find the central point of the design with a ruler and mark with the air-erasable pen. Place the metal washer in the middle of the design using the pen mark as a guide.

5 Using the embroidery thread, sew the washer in place with a couching stitch – space the stitches evenly around the ring and make sure you push the needle through all four layers.

6 With the same embroidery thread, hand sew a blanket stitch around the edge of the design, through all four layers.

7 To make the brooch more stable, use the template to cut another circle of felt and place this underneath the design. Using a different coloured embroidery thread, hand sew a running stitch through all the layers, about 1cm (½in) in from the edge, placing the stitches in the gaps between the blanket stitches.

8 Using a different thread, sew seven seed stitches spaced evenly around and radiating out from the metal washer – to get the spacing even, mark where to stitch with the air-erasable pen first.

9 Add a ring of small beads, positioning them between the seed stitches using your beading needle and thread.

10 Using embroidery thread, stitch an appropriately sized button in the centre.

11 Attach the brooch finding (see page 7).

Make a statement

Use bright fabrics to make a gorgeous stand-out piece. For this version, a fabric dye was used to create a bright pink scrim, which makes a bold contrast against the lime green fabric.

Cupcake Brooch

Materials:

Lightweight fabric,
  cotton or calico,
  14 x 14cm (5½ x 5½in)

Decorative fabrics, two types

Machine threads

Double-sided tape

Hessian fabric

Neutral-coloured felt

Brooch finding

Tools:

Embroidery hoop,
  10cm (4in)

Fabric scissors

Sewing machine

Instructions:

1 Secure a piece of lightweight fabric in the embroidery hoop.

2 Using the templates on page 48, cut out the cupcake case and icing shapes using a different decorative fabric for each.

3 Place the cupcake case into the upside down hoop (see page 7).

4 Using a light-coloured thread, machine sew a zigzag stitch from the top left hand corner of the case, down the left hand side, across the bottom and back up the right hand side – stop at the the top. Try to get the zigzag as close to the edge as you can. Prepare your machine for free machine embroidery (see page 7), then stitch up and down the cupcake case creating the effect of the paper creases.

5 Position the fabric icing shape so that it overlaps the top of the cupcake case. Using a red thread and starting at the top of the shape, stitch around the inside edge twice to secure it in place. When you get back to the top for the second time, free machine embroider a cherry shape by sewing round and round in circles, varying the size each time.

6 Cut the thread and then free machine embroider a little heart design in the bottom right hand corner of the cupcake case.

7 Cut the threads and take the fabric out of the embroidery hoop. Cut around the design leaving a 1cm (½in) wide border of the base lightweight fabric.

8 Place a small piece of double-sided tape on the back of the design and place it onto a piece of hessian. Cut around the hessian leaving a border just under 1cm (½in) wide. Now place the design onto a larger piece of felt.

9 Using a light-coloured thread, free machine embroider around the edge of the cupcake design – follow the line previously sewn around the top and sides of the icing, and sew inside the zigzag stitching on the case – securing all four layers together.

10 Cut the bottom felt layer to match the size of the hessian.

11 Attach the brooch finding (see page 7).

> **Tip: stitching tips**
> If your sewing machine struggles to stitch through all the layers in step nine, hand sew instead, keeping as close to the cupcake design as possible.

Decorative details

Try adding extra interest with a cute little button for the cherry and beads to fill the heart shape. If you are having a tea party with friends, why not turn it into a fun crafty session and make little cupcake brooches? They could also be used to decorate children's party bags.

Bridal Corsage

Materials:

Neutral-coloured felt

Lace

Wide organza ribbon,
7.5cm (3in) wide

Fine net

Cotton thread

Metallic thread

Decorative button

Brooch finding

Tools:

Air-erasable pen

Circular object with a diameter
of about 6cm (2¼in)

Fabric scissors

Hand sewing needle

Dress pins

Instructions:

1 On a piece of neutral-coloured felt, draw around your circular object with an air-erasable pen. Cut out the circle – this will be the base fabric on which you stitch your layers.

2 Cut a length of lace 40cm (16in) long and 5cm (2in) wide. Cut a length of thread, double it over and tie a double knot at the end. Stitch a small running stitch by hand along the entire length of the lace, approximately 0.5cm (¼in) from one edge – stitch along the less decorative edge if the lace has one.

3 Once you have stitched to the end, gather the lace by pulling the two ends of the thread together – manipulate the lace to create a tightly gathered circle. Tie the two thread ends together with a double knot to secure.

4 Place the gathered lace circle onto a piece of fine net and cut a net circle about 0.5cm (¼in) larger all round than the lace.

5 Lay the circle of net on top of the felt and then position the gathered lace circle on top. Using the cotton thread, sew all three layers together with about six stab stitches, evenly spaced around the gathered centre.

6 Cut a length of wide organza ribbon 35cm (14in) long and 7cm (2¾in) wide. Fold the ribbon in half lengthways and pin along the open edge to secure. As in step two, sew a small running stitch along the entire length, approximately 0.5cm (¼in) from the open edge. Once you have stitched to the end, remove the pins and gather the organza ribbon by pulling the two ends of the thread together. Manipulate the ribbon to create another gathered circle.

7 Place this layer on top of the lace, and secure it using another six stab stitches.

8 Cut a circular piece of lace slightly larger than your chosen button. Position it in the centre of the design, place the button on top and stitch it into place.

9 Using a metallic thread, sew a loose running stitch all around the edge of the net. Tie the two ends together with a double knot and cut off the excess thread.

10 Attach the brooch finding (see page 7).

Something borrowed

A wonderful wedding tradition is for the bride to have something borrowed with her on the day that symbolises happiness. This corsage provides a great opportunity to secure something borrowed to the centre. It may be your Grandma's brooch or a locket with a treasured little something inside. Be creative and make something extra special for the memorable day.

Vintage Lace Corsage

Materials:

Neutral-coloured felt

Lace

Cotton thread

Ribbon, two types

Medium button

Small button

Brooch finding

Tools:

Air-erasable pen

Circular object with a
diameter of about
6cm (2¼in)

Fabric scissors

Hand sewing
needle

Instructions:

1 On a piece of neutral-coloured felt, draw
around your circular object with an air-erasable pen.
Cut out the circle – this will be the base fabric on
which you stitch your layers.

2 Measure and cut a length of lace 40cm (16in) long and
about 5cm (2in) wide. Cut a length of thread, double it over and
tie a double knot at the end. Stitch a small running stitch along the entire
length of the lace, approximately 0.5cm (¼in) from one edge – stitch along
the less decorative edge if the lace has one.

3 Once you have stitched to the end, gather the lace by pulling the two ends
of the thread together – manipulate the lace to create a tightly gathered
circle. Tie the two thread ends together with a double knot to secure.

4 Cut another length of lace 30cm (12in) long and 4cm (1½in) wide; follow
steps two and three to make another gathered circle.

5 Place the lace circles on top of each other – smallest on the top – and
position them on top of the circular felt. Using the needle and thread, sew
all three layers together with about six stab stitches, evenly spaced around
the gathered centre.

6 Measure and cut two pieces of ribbon 12cm (5in) long and fold them
in half. Place the two open ends on top of each other and create an
upside down 'V' shape. Use a couple of stitches about 1cm (½in) from
the ends to secure the four layers.

7 Place the two buttons on top of each other, with the smallest
on the top, and stitch them onto the ribbon ends.

8 Place the buttons at the centre of the lace corsage and stitch
through all the layers and the buttons, securing them in place.

9 Attach the brooch finding (see page 7).

Vintage elegance

*Varying the type of lace can make a big difference to the feel.
Here, a softer lace has been used with a textured ribbon and
shell button resulting in a lovely vintage feel. This combination
could easily be adjusted and turned into a bridal hair clip.*

Silk Corsage

Materials:

Neutral-coloured felt

Medium-weight silk fabric

Cotton thread

Lace

Button

Embroidery thread

Brooch finding

Tools:

Circular object with a
    diameter of about
    6cm (2¼in)

Air-erasable pen

Fabric scissors

Dress pins

Hand sewing needle

Embroidery needle

Instructions:

1 On a piece of neutral-coloured felt, draw around your circular object with an air-erasable pen. Cut out the circle – this will be the base fabric on which you stitch your layers.

2 Measure and cut a length of silk fabric 1m (40in) long and 8cm (3⅛in) wide. Fold the silk in half lengthways and pin along the open edge to secure.

3 Take a long piece of doubled thread and knot it at the end. Sew a small hand running stitch along the entire length, approximately 0.5cm (¼in) from the open edge.

4 Once you have stitched to the end, gather the silk by pulling the two ends of the thread together. Manipulate the silk to create a well-gathered length.

5 Once you have ruched the silk to about half its original length, start to manipulate it into a spiral shape. The medium-weight silk fabric will keep its shape nicely and won't spring out of shape.

6 Once you have created a spiral you are happy with, lay it on top of the circle of felt created in step one. Using a needle and cotton thread, add lots of little stab stitches working from the bottom coming up through the felt and silk. Try to stitch following the spiral shape but take care to only stitch the lower layers of silk so you cannot see the stitches from the front.

7 Cut a piece of lace slightly larger than your chosen button. Stitch both the button and lace to the centre of the corsage using embroidery thread.

8 Attach the brooch finding (see page 7).

Brilliant buttons

If you have lots of buttons to choose from it's always fun to experiment with the effects of layering different types and colours. This design is a little more playful in colour, too, with the top button matching the bright pink scrim.

Felt Corsage

Materials:

Felt

Cotton thread

Embroidery thread

Button

Brooch finding

Tools:

Air-erasable pen

Circular object with a
    diameter of about
    4cm (1½in)

Fabric scissors

Hand sewing needle

Embroidery needle

Instructions:

1 Measure and cut eight lengths of felt, 11cm (4½in) long and 1cm (½in) wide.

2 On another piece of felt, draw around your circular object with an air-erasable pen. Cut out the circle – this will be the base fabric on which you stitch your layers.

3 Fold two lengths of felt and place them over the circular piece with the open ends touching each other in the centre, creating a horizontal line. With a double thickness of cotton thread, stitch both pieces into place with a few basic stitches. Don't worry about being neat as this area will not be seen.

4 Fold another two lengths of felt and place them on top of the previous ones, this time vertically. Again, the open ends should be touching each other in the centre. Secure in place with a few more stitches.

5 Repeat steps three and four twice more, this time positioning the lengths of felt diagonally so that the eight 'spokes' are equally spaced.

6 Measure and cut another eight lengths of felt, this time 8cm (3⅛in) long and 1cm (½in) wide.

7 Repeat steps three to five, this time making sure that these shorter lengths of felt sit in the gaps between the longer ones.

8 Using the embroidery thread, sew a large button into the centre of the design, pushing the needle through all the layers of fabric.

9 Attach the brooch finding (see page 7).

Colour explosion

Make the construction of this corsage even more interesting by mixing up the felt colours. This explosion of colour will have real impact worn on a dark jacket.

Found Objects Corsage

Materials:

Neutral-coloured felt

Light or medium-weight decorative fabric, two types

Embroidery thread

Coloured cotton fabric

30mm (1¼in) cover button

Small metal washer

Ribbon

Found objects, such as springs, nuts, tiny buttons, safety pins and beads

Brooch finding

Tools:

Air-erasable pen

Circular object with a diameter of about 7cm (2¾in)

Fabric scissors

Hand sewing needle

Pliers

Craft glue gun (optional)

Embroidery needle

Instructions:

1 On a piece of neutral-coloured felt, draw around your circular object with an air-erasable pen. Cut out the circle – this will be the base fabric on which you stitch your layers.

2 Measure and cut a length of decorative fabric 40cm (16in) long and 5cm (2in) wide. Cut a length of thread, double it over and tie a double knot at the end. Sew a small running stitch along the entire length of fabric approximately 0.5cm (¼in) from one edge.

3 Once you reach the other end, gather the fabric by pulling the two ends of the thread together. Manipulate the fabric to create a tightly gathered circle. Tie the ends of the thread together with a double knot to secure.

4 Repeat steps two and three with a second piece of decorative fabric measuring 26cm (10½in) long and 4cm (1½in) wide.

5 Place the gathered fabric circles on top of each other – with the smallest on top and the two 'joins' in the gathered circles aligned – and place them onto the circle of felt. Using the needle and thread, sew approximately six stab stitches around the central point – through all the layers – to secure.

6 Create the decorative cover button using the coloured cotton fabric; use the instructions provided to cut the correct size circle. Position the small metal washer in the centre of the fabric and stitch it in place using a couching stitch.

7 Carefully fold the fabric around the button following the instructions. Once in place, secure the cover button back. Attach the covered button to the centre of the design with a series of eight stab stitches: bring the needle through from the back of the brooch, catch the edge of the cover button fabric and then take it back through the layers. Alternatively, glue the covered button in place using a craft glue gun.

8 Cut a piece of ribbon 11cm (4½in) long and fold it at the centre point to create an upside down 'V' shape. Trim the ends at an angle to prevent them fraying. Stitch the ribbon into position just under the cover button using a couple of stab stitches, covering the 'joins'.

9 Cut a length of embroidery thread 30cm (12in) long. Using an embroidery needle, thread lots of different found objects onto it until you have filled a length of about 10cm (4in). Using the bottom object as an anchor, take the thread back up through the centre of all the other objects. Tie two knots as close to the top object as possible to secure. Thread back onto the needle and stitch into place just under the cover button.

10 Attach the brooch finding (see page 7).

Wintry wool

The use of lightweight wools works exceptionally well with this design and looks gorgeous worn on a winter coat or jacket. Raid charity shops for old clothing that you can deconstruct and turn into something funky. Old skirts, shirts and trousers can all be cut up and given a new lease of life.

Templates – shown at actual size

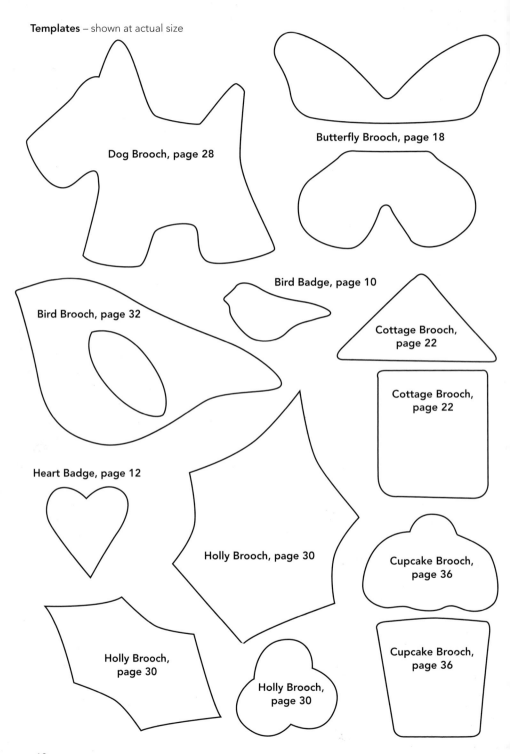

Dog Brooch, page 28

Butterfly Brooch, page 18

Bird Badge, page 10

Bird Brooch, page 32

Cottage Brooch, page 22

Cottage Brooch, page 22

Heart Badge, page 12

Holly Brooch, page 30

Cupcake Brooch, page 36

Holly Brooch, page 30

Holly Brooch, page 30

Cupcake Brooch, page 36